101 SILLY SUMMERTIME JOKES

by Stephanie Calmenson
Illustrated by Don Orehek

SCHOLASTIC INC.
New York Toronto London Auckland Sydney

ISBN 0-590-42556-0

Copyright © 1989 by Stephanie Calmenson.
Illustrations copyright © 1989 by Scholastic Inc.
All rights reserved. Published by Scholastic Inc.

24 23 22 21 20 19 18   6 7 8 9/9

Printed in the U.S.A.   01

First Scholastic printing, June 1989

101 SILLY SUMMERTIME JOKES

CAMP CRACK-UPS

Counselor: Now this is a dogwood
  tree.
Camper: How can you tell?
Counselor: By its bark.

Counselor: Why do bees hum?
Eddie: They don't know the words.

Camp Counselor: How did you get that horrible swelling on your nose?

Jimmy: I bent over to smell a brose.

Camp Counselor: There's no *b* in rose.

Jimmy: There was in this one.

Nature Counselor: Birds, though small, are remarkable creatures. For example, what can a bird do that I can't do?

Susie: Take a bath in a teacup.

**A boy wrote this letter home
from camp:**

Dear Mom and Dad:
   Gue$$ what I need? Plea$e $end
$ome $oon.

                         Be$t wi$he$,
                         Your $on $ammy

His parents wrote back:

Dear Sammy:
   NOthing much is happening here.
Please write aNOther letter soon.
Bye for NOw.

                         Love,
                         Mom and Dad

What happened to the camper who swallowed a flashlight?

He hiccuped with delight.

When should you wear a bathing suit to go horseback riding?

When you're riding a seahorse.

Camper: What has six eyes, ten arms, is six feet tall, and green all over?

Counselor: I don't know.

Camper: I don't know either, but there's one right outside our tent.

WHALE OF A TIME

What do you do with a blue whale?

Cheer him up.

Meg: What is the difference between a chocolate chip cookie and a whale?

Peg: Did you ever try dunking a whale in your milk?

If a psychiatrist charged $100 a visit, how much would she charge a whale for three visits?

Thirteen hundred dollars. That's $300 for the three visits and $1,000 for a new couch.

Edna: They say swimming is one of the best exercises for keeping the body slim and trim.

Harry: Oh really? Did you ever see a whale?

SOMETHING FISHY

First Fish: Have your eyes ever
  been checked?
Second Fish: No, they've always
  been gray.

Sidney: Have you ever seen a
  man-eating fish?
Ned: Sure.
Sidney: Where?
Ned: In a seafood restaurant.

How do you communicate with a fish?

Drop him a line.

What do you call a fish with two knees?

A *two-knee fish.*

What did the boy fish say to the girl fish?

Let's cut school and go for a swim.

Who performs operations at the fish hospital?

The head sturgeon.

Frank: What fish is the best
   singer?
Hank: A tuna fish.

How do you stop a fish from
smelling?

Hold its nose.

Nan: What part of a fish weighs the most?

Fran: Its scales.

HOT HINKY PINKYS

What do you call a talkative crab?

A *gabby crabby*.

What do you call sunspots shaped
like a rabbit?

A *sunny bunny*.

What do you get from a friendly bug?

A *bug hug*.

What do you call a traffic tie-up by the shore?

A clam jam.

What do you get from a crab
wearing boxing gloves?

A crab jab.

What do you call a flea who
vacations at the beach?

A sea flea.

What do you call a boring bird at
the shore?

A dull gull.

What does a fish make before blow-
ing out the candles on his birthday
cake?

A fish wish.

DOCTOR, DOCTOR

Patient: Doctor, something is
wrong with me. I keep thinking
I'm a frog.
Doctor: How long has this been
going on?
Patient: Since I was a tadpole.

Camper: Doctor, that ointment
you gave me makes my arm
smart.
Camp Doctor: In that case, rub
some on your head.

Sally: We've got to get my little brother to the doctor!

Willy: Why?

Sally: He swallowed a frog! He could croak any minute.

Patient: Doctor, I think corn is growing out of my ears.

Doctor: Why, so it is. How did this happen?

Patient: Beats me. I planted radishes.

DOPEY DUOS

Jim: How did you find the weather when you were on vacation?

Slim: It was easy. I went outside and there it was.

Wife: I've got good news. We've saved enough money for us to go cross-country this summer.

Husband: That's wonderful. When are we leaving?

Wife: As soon as we've saved enough money to get back.

Mother: How did you get that black eye?

Jim: I was hit with tomatoes.

Mother: Tomatoes gave you a black eye?

Jim: They were in a can.

Jane: Marshmallows are a very useful food.

Judy: How's that?

Josie: You can powder your nose with them before toasting them.

YOURS TRULY

Yours till Cats-kill Mountains.

Yours till Bear Mountain gets
dressed.

Yours till the ocean wears rubber
pants to keep its bottom dry.

WHAT? WHAT? WHAT?

What did the big Fourth-of-July firecracker say to the little Fourth-of-July firecracker?

My pop's bigger than your pop.

What is black and white and red all over?

A sunburned zebra.

What is gray, has four legs, and a
trunk?

A mouse going on vacation.

What do you call a carousel with no brakes?

A *merry-go-round-round-round-round-round.* . . .

What happens to an air conditioner when you pull its plug?

It loses its cool.

What does a three-headed frog say?

WHAT'S THE QUESTION?

Answer: *Buzz. Buzz. Buzz. Plop.*
Question: What is the sound of a
  bee laughing its head off?

Answer: *A towel.*
Question: What gets wetter the
  more it dries?

Answer: *He wanted to get up oily
  in the morning.*
Question: Why did the fisherman
  sleep in the salad dressing?

Answer: *A coconut on vacation.*
Question: What is brown, hairy, and wears sunglasses?

FUN WITH FIVES

Bob: If you found two five-dollar bills in the pocket of your bathing suit, what would you have?

Rob: Someone else's bathing suit.

Counselor: Joey, if you had five pieces of candy, and Oscar asked you for one, how many pieces would you have left?

Joey: Five.

Psychiatrists tell us that one out of five people is mentally ill. So check your bunkmates — if four of them seem to be all right, you're the one.

PLAY BALL!

What has eighteen legs and catches flies?

A baseball team.

Why did the ballplayer bring rope to the game?

He wanted to tie the score.

First Baseman: Why was the singer invited to the ball game?
Second Baseman: I don't know. Why?
First Baseman: She had perfect pitch.

First Baseman: They just fired the
outfielder.
Pitcher: Why?
First Baseman: He was such a
nice guy, he wouldn't even catch
a fly.

Doctor: What did you dream about last night?

Patient: Baseball.

Doctor: And what did you dream about the night before?

Patient: Baseball.

Doctor: Don't you ever dream about anything else?

Patient: What, and miss my turn at bat?

Junior: Dad, I can't find my baseball mitt.

Dad: Look in the car.

Junior: I did, but I couldn't find it.

Dad: Did you try the glove compartment?

FUNNY FARM

The Smiths visited a farm on their vacation. They had a great time, except for the pigs. They didn't like the pigs' snorting.

The next year, they wrote a letter to the farmer and asked if he still had pigs.

"Nope," wrote the farmer. "We haven't had any pigs since you were here."

What is heavier: a hundred pounds of feathers or a hundred pounds of sand?

Neither. They both weigh a hundred pounds.

When is a duck twenty feet tall?

When he's on stilts.

City Slicker: There sure are a lot of flies around here. Don't you ever shoo them?

Farmer: No. We just let them go barefoot.

City Slicker: So, how many bushels of apples do you think you'll get from that tree?

Farmer: None.

City Slicker: That's too bad.

Farmer: No, it isn't. That's a pear tree.

Where do cows go on vacation?

Moo York.

What do they do when they get there?

Go to the moo-seum, then catch a moo-vie.

Where did the farmer take his pigs on a sunny Sunday afternoon?

On a pignic.

WHO'S THERE?

Knock, knock.
Who's there?
Dewey.
Dewey who?
Dewey have to go into the water
   today?

Knock, knock.
Who's there?
Shrimp.
Shrimp who?
Shrimp's too short to reach the
   doorbell.

Knock, knock.

Who's there?

Harriet.

Harriet who?

Harriet all the watermelon, and
there's none left for us.

Knock, knock.
Who's there?
Amos.
Amos who?
Amos-quito just bit me!

Knock, knock.
Who's there?
Crab.
Crab who?
Crab your suit, and we'll go for a
    swim.

SUMMER BEST-SELLERS

I Was a Bathing Beauty Queen
  by Teuton Tilly

Learn To Swim in Thirty Seconds
  by Bea A. Fish

Beach Vacations Around the World
  by Yul B. Sandy

How To Treat Poison Ivy
  by I. M. Itchy

Take Me Out to the Ball Game
  by Hedda Homer

Noises in the Woods
  by Izzy A. Bear

Insects Are Your Friends
  by Amos Keetah

The Cookout Cookbook
  by Burntoo A. Crisp

My Summer Romance
  by Luv E. Duvey

CORNY JOKES

What does a worm do in a corn-field?

It goes in one ear and out the other.

Baby Corn: Mommy, where did I come from?
Mother Corn: The stalk brought you.

What has ears, but can't hear?

A cornstalk.

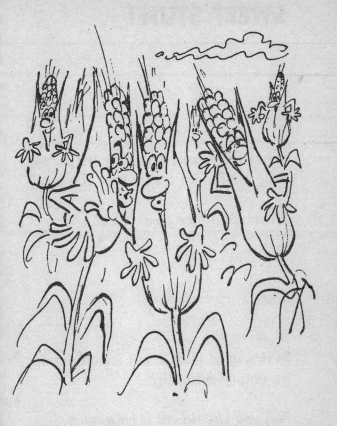

Why should you never tell a secret
in a cornfield?

Because corn has ears and cornstalk.

SWEET STUFF!

What happened when the little boy dropped his ice cream into the pool?

He made an ice cream float.

Is it a good idea to eat ice cream on an empty stomach?

No, you should eat it on a stick.

What most resembles half a berry?

The other half.

What did one strawberry say to the other?

If you weren't so fresh, we wouldn't be in this jam.

Radish: Lettuce get married tonight!
Cucumber: No, no! We cantaloupe.
Radish: Oh, please, honeydew.

WAITER, WAITER

Diner: There's a fly drowning in
my lemonade!
Waiter: Quick, give him mouth-to-
mouth resuscitation!

Diner: Waiter, do you serve crabs
here?
Waiter: Sit down. We serve anyone.

Diner: Waiter, there's a fly in my rum raisin ice cream.

Waiter: No trouble, madam. I'll take it back and exchange it for a raisin.

Waiter: Have you tried the fish, sir?

Diner: Yes — and I found it guilty.

Diner: What is this fly doing in my ice cream?

Waiter: I believe it's downhill skiing, sir.

BUG FUN

Bess: What do you need to know to teach a grasshopper tricks?

Tess: More than the grasshopper.

What weighs one thousand pounds, is orange and black, flies, and hums?

Two five-hundred-pound bumble-bees.

What is green, has six legs, and can jump over your head?

A grasshopper with the hiccups.

What has four legs and flies?

A horse in the summertime.

What letter is an insect?

B.

Ann: What's the difference between a bumblebee and a mattababy?
Sue: What's a mattababy?
Ann: Why, nothing. What's the matter with you?

CALLING ALL CATS

What happens to a cat who drinks too much lemonade?

It turns into a sourpuss.

What do you call a cat at the beach?

Sandy Claws.

If there were ten cats in a boat, and
one jumped out, how many cats
would be left?

None. They're copycats.

TONGUE TWISTERS

Sally sells seashells by the sea-
  shore.
Surely she will sell some seashells
  soon.

A swim well swum is a well-swum
  swim.

Six shifty sharks shouted sharply.

Five fat frogs fly past fast.
The fattest frog flies past fastest.

We shall surely see the sun shine
  soon.

Fred's friend Fran fries fresh fish.

Ten tiny turtles tickling toes.

BEACH-BOUND BIGGIES

What time is it when an elephant jumps off a diving board?

Time to get a new diving board.

How do you fit six elephants into a motorboat?

Put three in the front seat and three in the back.

Sunbathing Giraffe: Why are you looking over your sunglasses instead of through them?
Sunbathing Elephant: I don't want to wear them out.

Why did the twin elephants get thrown off the beach?

They had only one pair of trunks.

How do you make an elephant
float?

*Put two scoops of ice cream, some
milk, and some soda water into a
glass. Add one elephant.*

If you saw nine elephants walking
down the beach with red bathing
suits, and one elephant walking
down the beach with a green
bathing suit, what would this
prove?

*That nine out of ten elephants wear
red bathing suits.*

TOM SWIFTIES

"I'd like another hot dog," said Tom frankly.

"This ice cream is for you," said Jill sweetly.

"I hear an owl," Dan hooted.

"Let's go sailing," said Tom breezily.

"I want to ride a pony," said Tom hoarsely.

"Listen to those pigs," Tom snorted.

"It must be one hundred degrees in the shade!" said Tom hotly.

"I am not going swimming!" said Tom dryly.

"This lemonade tastes terrible," said Tom sourly.

"What is this bone doing in my fish chowder?" asked Tom crabbily.

WHY? WHY? WHY?

Why did the firefly get bad grades
in school?

He wasn't very bright.

Why did the cow cross the road?

The chicken was on vacation.

Why did Humpty Dumpty have a
great fall?

*He wanted to make up for a bad
summer.*

Why is a dog so hot in the summer?

Because he wears a coat and pants.

Why is tennis such a noisy game?

Because each player raises a racquet.

Why should you keep the letter **M**
out of your freezer?

*So you don't get **m**ice.*

Why do spiders make good out-
fielders?

They catch flies.

Why did the little boy put suntan
lotion on the chicken?

Because he liked dark meat.

COOL GHOULS

What is a monster's favorite
summer drink?

Ghoul-aid.

Monster Child: Mommy, may I
eat my corn on the cob with my
fingers?
Monster Mother: No. Eat your
fingers separately.

Monster Child: Mother, I hate my
counselor.
Monster Mother: Then just eat
your salad.

What do ghosts do at an amusement park?

They ride the roller-ghoster.

What is white, turning blue?

A ghost underwater, holding its breath.

Why didn't the werewolf get sunburned at the beach?

He was wearing his moon-tan lotion.

Where do goblins like to go swimming?

Lake Eerie.

What flowers grow in a ghost's garden?

Marighouls.

What is a vampire's favorite fruit?

A *neck-tarine*.

What do you get when you cross a mosquito with a vampire.

A *very itchy neck*.

What boats do vampires like best?

Blood vessels.

SHARP SHARKS

First Sardine: How do you hug a hungry shark?

Second Sardine: Very carefully.

Meg: Do you think we should swim here? I heard there were crocodiles.

Peg: Don't worry. The sharks scare them away.

What do you say to a forty-ton shark with razor-sharp teeth, who is listening to his headphones with the volume turned way up?

Anything you want. He can't hear you.

Lois: What would you do if you saw a big, hungry, man-eating shark?

Ned: Pray it didn't see me.

Hank: I can lift a shark with one hand.

Al: I don't believe you.

Hank: Get me a shark with one hand, and I'll show you.

Boy: A shark just bit my leg!

Doctor: Did you put anything on it?

Boy: No. He liked it the way it was.

What do you get if you cross a
shark with a Boy Scout?

*A shark that helps old ladies across
the ocean.*

When is a shark like a cute little bunny rabbit?

When it's wearing its cute little bunny-rabbit suit.

What does a shark eat with peanut butter?

Jellyfish.

What kind of noise do you get when you cross a shark with a poodle?

A shark bark.

SEASIDE SILLIES

Lobster: What did the high tide say to the low tide?

Crab: 'Lo, tide.

Lobster: What did the low tide say to the high tide?

Crab: Hi, tide.

Lobster: Then what did they say?

Crab: Nothing. They just waved.

Which are the strongest creatures
in the ocean?

Mussels.

Susie: A crab just bit off my toe!
Donald: Which one?
Susie: I don't know. All crabs look
  alike to me.

First Dolphin: Hey, you just cut
  me off!
Second Dolphin: Sorry. I didn't do
  it on porpoise.

What did the boy octopus say to the girl octopus?

I want to hold your hand, hand, hand, hand, hand, hand, hand, hand.

She: You remind me of the ocean.

He: You mean I'm deep and strong and wild?

She: No, you make me sick.

Little Boy: Daddy, do you think clams are happy?

Father: Have you ever heard one complain?

What is a lobster after it is five
years old?

Six years old.

What did the shrimp say when the
lobster stole his food?

Gee, you're shellfish!

How do you know clams are lazy?

They are always in their beds.

Why does the ocean roar?

*You would, too, if there were
lobsters in your bed.*

What did the beach say as the tide
came in?

Long time, no sea.

Yours till the ocean waves.